This book depicts everything that Kail truly is: raw, relatable and full of heart. To be able to watch her navigate through life and for her to be able to share a side of herself that not many witness is amazing. I'm proud to call her a friend and feel blessed to share motherhood with such a beautiful soul.

–Lindsie Chrisley

To be a woman in today's society, so critical. So judgemental is a task worthy of an Emmy. To be a woman in today's society, while raising children, is a task worthy of a Golden Globe. To be a woman in today's society, while raising children, being in the public eye, and living your truth, is a task worthy of presidential honor. As a woman, one of the most powerful attributes she can possess is self-acceptance. It is only then that she can do ANYTHING; she can defeat all odds. She is a rarity, a jewel more precious than Gold. She harbors a love so deep, and so pure, that very few are lucky to experience her passion. I am one of the few, that has been blessed to experience all of the above from Kail. It's a beautiful thing to watch her be bold enough to embrace her vulnerability, and best of all, share her love with no boundaries, no limits, with the world.

–Monica Slaughter

Kail's transparency and vulnerability even in the most sensitive and difficult times in her life have always inspired me. This book invites people into a part of her life that only a few of us have known. To see her resilience through struggle, as well as her deep love for her children will give readers a greater appreciation for the incredible woman Kail is. I couldn't be more proud of the amazing, strong and determined person she is! I am beyond grateful that I have the privilege of calling her my friend.

–Leah Messer

a letter of
LOVE

KAILYN LOWRY

13th & Joan books may be purchased for educational, business or
sales promotional use. For information, please email the Sales Depart-
ment at sales@13thandjoan.com.

First Edition
Library of Congress Cataloging-in-Publication Data has been applied for.
ISBN 978-1-7324712-9-0

TO MY

children & supporters

WHO HAVE BEEN

FOLLOWING MY JOURNEY & TO

anyone

WHO HAS GONE THROUGH

heartbreak.

Foreword

When I was asked to write the foreword for Kail's book, I was honored. As I wrote, I found it so hard to condense the almost six years we've been friends into a few paragraphs. There are so many layers of Kail that I wish everyone out there could see.

Kailyn Lowry, the girl from Teen Mom 2 that has three babies daddies; that's how many people love to refer to her. To me, she is Kailyn Rae, my best friend. She is one of the most amazing examples of a mother that I know. She is someone that I have looked up to for so many reasons as my confidant, and my soul sister.

The person that you see on TV is 99.9% not the same person I know. The 1% that you see on outtakes, the unseen moments of the show, when she's laughing and having fun with her kids, making smart ass comments about something, eating every carbohydrate in sight, or giving someone a tiny glimpse of her attitude; that's the girl that I know and love. Over the years, as her storyline has played out on TV, a lot of people have come to the conclusion that she is a man-hating, cheating, bitter, angry girl that's never grown up from the "16 and Pregnant" phase where the world met her.

I've had the privilege of watching Kailyn grow as a woman, a human, a mother, an entrepreneur, a student, and as a wife while she was married. I met Kailyn when she was married and a new mom of two after Lincoln was born. I watched her try and create the picture perfect family with a mom, dad, and two kids, because she craved that so badly herself after growing up in a broken home. Was she truly happy? No. However, she tried so hard to force herself to be. I watched as she tried to be the best wife she could after not having any example and also while also realizing the marriage she entered into was not ultimately meant for her. I watched as she struggled through breastfeeding Lincoln for a full year because she wanted to give him the best, and to be the best mom, no matter how tough it was and how draining it was on her mind and body.

Why does this matter? I've watched Kailyn sacrifice herself and her happiness time and time again to create the life she wanted when she was growing up. Has her past hardened her? Absolutely. Just like many of us out there, the past plays a role in who we become. The angry person she comes across as is not who she truly is. The thing about Kailyn that only a few who are closest to her know is that her first reaction to everything is anger. Whether she's sad, hurt, pissed or any other negative emotion, she comes across angry. It's her defense mechanism. The ones who know her understand what's going on under the surface. If I could think of a motto to describe Kailyn, it would be, "Get pissed first and cry about it later."

If you want to see her at her happiest, catch her with her kids. Her boys bring her so much joy. She'll tell anyone that she loves the chaos of having the three of them running around. Whether they're playing in the pool, relaxing while watching movies, or lying in her bed in the mornings, she lives for those moments. I tell everyone that Kailyn was born to be a mother. She doubts herself at times, but she really kills the mom game.

During her pregnancy with Lux was the lowest I've ever seen her in our friendship. Kailyn was struggling through relationship issues with Lux's dad and went through the majority of her pregnancy alone. And yes, she had her friends around, but she really believed she was finally going to have the family she wanted so badly with Lux's dad. She loved him and was in love with him. For the first time in her life, she thought she had found a once in a lifetime love. The saddest thing was watching my sister so happy to be bringing her rainbow baby into the world, but so depressed that she was doing it alone.

Kailyn made sure Isaac and Lincoln rarely saw how depressed she really was. She helped the boys get so excited for the baby. They asked her every day when Lux was going to be here? The strength it took for her to pretend like she wasn't dying inside when the boys were around was remarkable to watch. What you all saw while Kail was pregnant was her pissed off shell. You didn't see her falling into pieces behind closed doors because she couldn't understand why things didn't work out with Chris.

Now that Lux is here, I'm amazed by the growth I've seen in Kail. She made the transition to three look so easy that anyone could do it. She made sure the boys all had a chance to bond together, always having the three boys together when they're with her. Even while she dealt with the pain of all of Lux's first occurring without the family she envisioned, she always kept her priorities in check by being an amazing mom to her kids. All Kailyn wants is to raise happy boys that love each other and contribute their skill sets to society.

I've never met another individual as accepting as Kailyn. She practices that acceptance in her parenting. Her boys never have to question the amount of love she has for them. They will always know that she accepts them and will continue to accept them for who they are. She's open to them trying anything they can imagine. Isaac has said for years that he wants to be a paleontologist which Kailyn thinks is amazing. She doesn't care what Isaac wants to be; as long as he is happy, she'll support him and his brothers all the same.

Despite everything Kailyn has been through, her energy is incredible. She's the type of person you want to be around even while doing nothing. She's such a homebody even when she doesn't have the boys, and loves nothing more than curling up with some snacks while watching the ID channel. I feel badly for those of you who only know Kail from TV because you don't know the funny, smart, and caring person she really is.

I can't wait to continue watching the evolution of Kailyn. She has her incredible podcast going strong, a hair care line ready to launch and various other projects in the works. I have no idea how she balances motherhood, her businesses, and her friendships, but she figures it out along the way and does so well. I'm one of the lucky ones to be able to call her my best friend, and I can't wait for all the incredible things still left to come for Kailyn, Isaac, Lincoln, and Lux

Kristen,
soul sister

Acknowledgments

I'm thankful for my sons, who give me passion and purpose...a reason to write.

This book wouldn't be possible if it weren't for Ardre Orie and the entire 13th & Joan Publishing team. Ardre kept me writing when I didn't think I had anything left to say.

Thank you to Wendy Darling, Photography, for the cover shot and most of our family photos.

Thank you to Kristen Hook for my makeup!

Thanks to Becky for being there for me since Isaac was a toddler.

I'm also thankful for all of my supporters who have been with me from the beginning, as well as the new ones. You all have followed my journey and tried to understand why I do what I do.

Kail

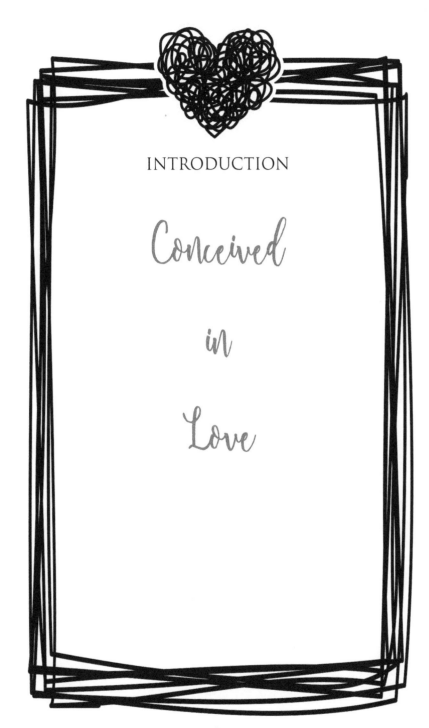

INTRODUCTION

Conceived

in

Love

In the end,

THE ONLY THING THAT WILL

matter

IS HOW WELL WE

HAVE MANAGED TO

love.

———♥———

Kailyn Lowry

've come to realize that everything that I do is conceived in love. At first, this book started as an apology letter to Lux, my third son. I felt so much guilt, regret, and sorrow for him after he was born. From the moment I found out that I was pregnant with Lux, I knew that I was never going to be able to work it out with his dad. I desperately wanted it to work. This has been one of the most painful internal battles that I have ever faced.

As I reflected on all that has happened over the years, I began to consider the fact that I couldn't make it work with any of my boys' dads, not just Lux. Although painful to admit, I came to a place where I recognized and acknowledged that I am the common denominator. Do you know how hard it is to admit to yourself that you've been the problem all along? It hurts like hell to know that all you've ever tried to do was to love, and it was to no avail. I never started a relationship with the intent of it ending. I have never given birth to a child who was not conceived in love. Everything inside of me has wanted to be both a giver and a receiver of love, but love has not always opened the door for me. At times, I've been so close to happiness that I felt like I could reach out and touch it, but none of it has been real or enough to withstand the test of time.

Today, I recognize that I am left to pick up the pieces of the mess that has been created in unfulfilled relationships, and most importantly, there is a need to repair the broken pieces of my heart. In doing so, I have only one wish: to be the best mom I can be. Picking up the pieces also means owning my truth.

It's important for me to write this book now because I'm still struggling. This is my reality. I want my kids to know that loving hasn't been easy, but I am trying my hardest for them. I will never give up because I want my boys to know that they were conceived in love and that they will always be loved by their dads and me. I'm also writing this book because I know that I am not alone. I know that there are others in the world who desire love as much as I do. I will never stop believing that true love exists and that it is out there for me. Being the love that I want my boys to find is always a sure thing. Love is not a word that describes; it is a word that acts. Everything that I have done and everything that I will do will always be conceived in love.

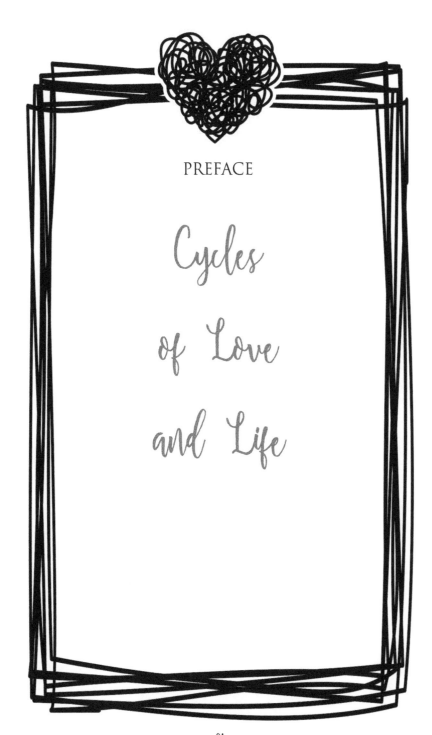

PREFACE

Cycles
of Love
and Life

LIFE IS SHORT. WE MUST

learn

TO NOT SPEND OUR

TIME AT WAR WITH

ourselves.

Kailyn Lowry

There is one thing that I know for sure: life goes through phases. Whether good or bad, I've learned that with each stage, our power lies in our ability to act in love. Anything else that we do won't yield the results that we want. All of us desire to be loved and understood. For me, love has been the one sentiment that has conquered everything that has ever happened, and believe me when I say that quite a bit has happened over the years. Through it all, I now recognize that every moment was a building block for a more solid foundation for my life. While we all search for a purpose on a daily basis and continue to question our reason for existence, I do know that we are all purposed to love. It may sound simple, but that's because it is.

Every phase of our lives leaves us with valuable stories to tell. Within these stories, we discover moments of passion, moments of pain, moments of power, moments of finding purpose, and the sweetest moment of all - poetic justice. These are the cycles of our lives.

Today, more than ever, I've come full circle in so many ways. I recognize the importance of telling my story in a way that has not yet been done. There are so many things that I have left unspoken for fear of what the world would think or how others may feel. It was a powerful revelation to decide to walk in my truth. I realized that my television portrayal had not sincerely told my story my way. I feel compelled to tell my truths to ensure that I leave a lasting legacy of love for my greatest accomplishment, my sons.

In the pages of this book, you will discover the passion, the pain, the power, the purpose, and the poetic justice revealed in the cycles of my life. I've spared no elements of the stories merged to reveal my deepest thoughts because there was no point in doing so. I no longer wish to water down pieces of my life to appease others. I no longer wish to create a storyline to keep others interested. I am only interested in the truth and ensuring that my boys have answers to the questions that they may have as they get older and learn about my life. If the truth sets us free, I'm preparing to spread my wings and fly. This is the truth, as told by me. This is my story, written my way.

Table of Contents

Love

HAS THE ABILITY TO

hurt

AND THE ABILITY TO

heal.

❤

Kailyn Lowry

ONE

I'm

Sorry...

FORGIVE ME.

I love you.

Kailyn Lowry

ove hurts like hell! It is not possible to love or to be loved and never experience hurt. It just doesn't work that way. When we realize that we've caused harm or hurt, love forces us to yield or to give an apology. If we are brave enough to love, we will inevitably get hurt.

Those of us who desire to love must be willing to heal our wounds and be willing to get back up and try it all again. For me, life has been a series of trial and error, and that's okay. I'm just one of those people who will keep trying until the day that I discover a love that doesn't end in pain. I want to be the source of love that I have always desired for myself.

Love can't be discovered without experiencing the unknown. In full transparency, I would say that I have made some mistakes along the way. Who hasn't? For those mistakes, I apologize. I will never apologize for trying my hand at love, but I do apologize for anyone who has ever gotten hurt during the process. What you've seen over the years was me trying to get it right. In my heart, I feel like only a portion of the truth was exposed.

Partial truths allow people to get hurt, especially children.

I must publicly apologize to my boys for some of the "stuff" in the media that they are going to read about me. I'm not sorry for doing the show, but I am sorry for not being fully aware of how things were produced. I am sorry for some of the things that have been done on the show. I haven't always made good choices. Many of my bad decisions, mixed with the production of a reality show, don't always air according to how things really happened. There were so many times that I didn't accurately show my feelings.

I have said some things on social media that were escalated in the tabloids. I have to face the truth one day. My boys are going to be able to google and find things about me that may not be favorable; however, those things don't define who I honestly am.

I want my boys to know that I am human, and I want them to know that I have made some mistakes, despite my best efforts. While I take full responsibility for my actions, I also recognize that I didn't ever have an example of a mother or father when I was growing up.

Since I didn't have a point of reference on how to love, I desperately want my boys to understand that I have tried to love them in the best way that I can.

I want to apologize to my fans. Sometimes, I feel as if I've not come across as true to who I am while on television. There have been times when I've appeared "cold" because I was scared to be transparent and opened. In some moments, I didn't want to cry or look a certain way, but in the end, it has backfired on me. I've looked at past seasons, and I think to myself that I am not the bitch that I appeared to be. I'm a compassionate person who is emotionally weak, but I often try to hide or shield myself from hurt. When I try to protect these emotions and not be opened and raw, I create a barrier between who people believe me to be and who I am. People hate me because they think that I am so heartless and calculated, but that's not me at all. I would give the shirt off my back to someone in need, however, not a lot of people realize that about me.

Sometimes, it's hard because I don't think that I always get to deal with the events that happen in my life in real time. If things about my personal life leak, it means that it's fair game for the show or for the media. I am human, and I have good and bad days like everyone else.

There are days when I'm tired, and I can't get out of bed. There are days when I am just doing the best that I can as a mom. I have tried to cover up what I may be going through at times just to film the show, but real life is happening around me. It is possible that I could be immersed in my feelings from a series of events that happened prior to the show, but while filming, it appears that I am numb to the world.

There are so many times when I am faced with scenarios where people treat me like I am just some character on a show, but I am a real person who wants nothing more than to connect with other real people. No matter what has happened, my heart is filled with nothing but love.

Today, I stand firmly in knowing that everything I have done was rooted in love. To those that I have hurt, I'm sorry.

Kail

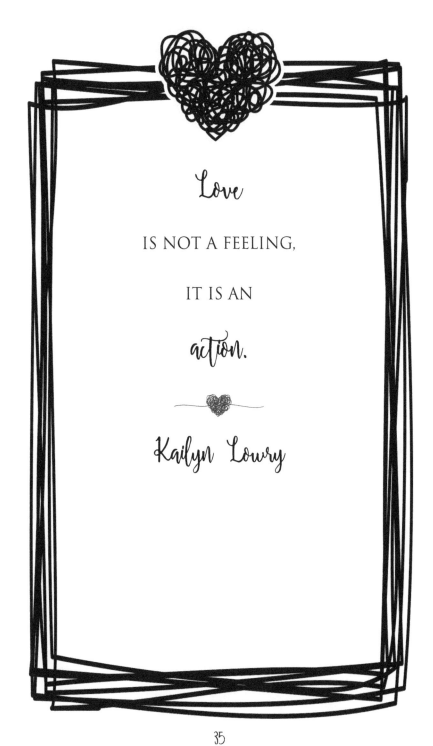

Love

IS NOT A FEELING,

IT IS AN

action.

Kailyn Lowry

TWO

Love

Is...

I was standing beneath the clouds, and the sun was shining on my face.

Far off in the distance, an angel called my name.

I turned to see his face, and I was blinded by the sun.

With eyes squinting in his direction, I heard him whisper "You're the chosen one."

"Chosen one for what? I'm just here to pass the time by.

"I had no intentions of putting my heart on the line."

Without warning, he began to speak again.

"You've been chosen to give and to be and to seek love, my friend."

Dazed and confused from his words, I began to speak again.

"Chosen to love? I have no meaning of the concept. It has caused me so much pain.

"Why would I be chosen to love? For me, love has never been the wind beneath my wings."

And in an instant, he began to speak again.

"Love is indeed the wind beneath our wings, the soft caress of happiness, and the warmth in our hearts. It doesn't brag or boast or keep score of the errors of our ways.

"Love is the sun shining on your face and the moon glowing at night.

"But we all too soon forget that love comes at a very costly price."

And in an instant, I interrupted with my thoughts.

"Love comes at a cost I'm not prepared to pay. So many people, places, and things have stood in my way. It's hard for me to believe that love has ever come to me or that it was willing to stay."

He began to speak once more, "You must trust the process and welcome the pain. Love without limits will shelter you from the rain. Love without rules or notions that make sense will come to you in the darkness and light your steps. Love is yours for the taking if only you would let it in. You must come to know that true love will find its way to you, the moment you learn to let go."

Just like that, the angel disappeared and I opened my eyes. It was in that moment that

I realized I was surrounded by love both great and small.

For in my search I had been given the greatest gift of all. The most profound expressions of love given unto me was to honor and protect little hearts brought into the world and to catch them before they fall.

Today when the angel calls my name in the distance, I hasten to answer "yes". I know that the essence of true love is rooted deeply in the heart that beats strongly within my chest.

True love must be given more than it will ever be received, for the purest love of my life was conceived inside of me.

Love

IS THE GIVER OF

life.

♥

Kailyn Lowry

THREE

Isaac

IF I CAN TEACH MY

CHILDREN TO OPEN THEIR

hearts

TOWARDS LOVE,

THEN I HAVE SERVED MY

purpose

IN THEIR LIVES.

Kailyn Lowry

The

Birth

of

Isaac

New life

IS AN OPEN DOOR TO NEW

beginnings.

❤

Kailyn Lowry

My water must have broken around five in the morning, but for whatever reason I thought I just didn't make it to the bathroom in time to pee. I cleaned myself up and went back to sleep. Jo was working with his mom in New Jersey at the time, so he was already a few hours into his day when I realized that I was having period like cramps. I called my mom, because who the hell else could I call? She left work and came to see what was going on, and she let me know that I was actually in labor. We called the doctor, and he told us to come to his office.

The doctor wasn't at his office near us; he was almost thirty minutes away. For whatever reason, that's where my mom started to drive. At this point, my contractions were four minutes apart. By the time we got into the elevator at the doctor's office, I felt a huge gush. We were left with no choice other than to go across the street to the hospital. We didn't know if my doctor worked there or if they had a mother/baby unit. Luckily, my doctor also worked at that hospital.

Now, I'm in labor for what seemed like forever. I didn't actually give birth until the evening. Throughout the whole process, there were so many people in the room. This was more than any hospital should have ever allowed. My mom, Jo's dad, brother, mother, and a ton of our friends were there, but the producers of MTV's *16 & Pregnant* arrived. They lie by the way. In order for them to be there, we had to tell the hospital staff that they were my cousins who wanted to film the birth. Looking back, that was kind of fucked up. Now that I have two other babies, I realize that I didn't get to have a peaceful birth for Isaac. He was literally born into chaos. The room was pure chaos. After thirteen entire hours of labor, I heard Jo say, "It's a boy," but I didn't know what to think or what to feel. My emotions were in pure chaos just like the atmosphere in the room.

The

Passion

She loved

SO MUCH THAT SHE

SOMETIMES FORGOT

To love herself.

Kailyn Lowry

I can honestly say that I have very little regret about my relationship with Jo. We were very young and looking for love.

When we first met, he didn't talk much, and he was a little mysterious. He didn't put himself out there too much, and it made me curious about him. We fell in love quickly. While we were together, things were hot and heavy. Everyone else might have known that we were not good for each other, but we never stopped to notice. We started a cycle of breaking up and getting back together within the first year. If that's not a red flag that the relationship is in danger, then I don't know what is.

Today, I can't place my finger on exactly what did work for us. You simply outgrow some people. Jo and I were no different. He was a good person. We just were not made for each other.

The

Pain

IT IS POSSIBLE TO

BREAK YOUR OWN

heart.

❤

Kailyn Lowry

ou think you know pain until life blindsides you.

Jo wanted to move back to his hometown in New Jersey, but there was no way I wanted that. I was staying put, and that was final. On the same hand, the relationship between Jo and me couldn't work amidst the cheating. Both of us wanted to go in different directions. We didn't want to be together, but we also didn't want to see the other person with anyone else. It seemed like it would be never ending.

When I got my first real paycheck from the show, I blew it. I got a more reliable car, a Jeep Liberty, from Jo's dad, and I moved into a one bedroom apartment. That was around the same time I started to think things would look up for me. I only completed one year of school, and I thought maybe dental assisting would be better. I did dental assisting for a while, and around this time, I met Javi. I'm not here to bash him or say he's a bad guy, but when I look back, I feel like I rushed into things. Jo warned me, but I felt like I wanted to fix everything. I had a child at a young age; therefore, I felt like getting married to someone would be a resolve. The regret is weird for me because obviously none of us would be where we are now if it were not for those choices. I wanted to lift Isaac up (with Javi), but in the end, I felt like I turned around and let him down. I don't want Isaac or any of my children to ever rush into relationships because of the pressure around them or to achieve a certain image of how life should be. If it's right, you won't have to rush. After the first year, the relationship was extremely toxic, but we were already married. This was a lesson for me but at the expense of my child.

The

Power

SOMETIMES YOU HAVE

TO STAND IN THE

ashes

OF WHO YOU

once were.

Kailyn Lowry

There is nothing worse than feeling out of control and powerless. This was my reality, and it felt like there was nothing that I could do about it. When I realized that all the power that I needed was inside of me, I made a choice to create opportunities for myself based on what was in front of me. Life was no longer about me and my wants and needs. I was now living to ensure that Isaac never had anything but love. The thought of his smile fueled me!

As I reflect on all that has transpired, I can say with certainty that Isaac changed my life. He was six pounds and four ounces of life in my hands. He had a few health complications, and he wouldn't latch to nurse, but I was instantly overwhelmed – both good and bad. I remember my friends coming to visit us in the hospital, and I was so tired I couldn't even love the visits. Leaving the hospital terrified me even more because no one was able to take off work to help me. I was thrown into motherhood full throttle from day one. Jo hadn't stayed one night with me in the hospital.

I was thankful because Isaac was a good baby. He went everywhere with me, and we did everything together. He even came to my college orientation. Within six to eight months, his dad and I split for good. I was connected to Isaac more than ever before. I felt like it was him and me against the world. We eventually moved into a one bedroom apartment. I was collecting food stamps, and I never seemed to have a reliable car. I barely got the rent paid on time, but we made it work. We lived there for an entire year while I was working at an Italian restaurant, a sporting goods store, and going to school full time. Coming home to Isaac and knowing that I could make it all work for him kept me going.

I know that people say things like that all the time, but Isaac saved me. If I didn't have him, I would have realized the hard times that were in front of me. This could have taken me down a completely different path, more like my mother's. We celebrated Isaac's first birthday in that apartment. The day was not completely filled with excitement, but it was filled with tons of love. From the homemade cupcakes to the countless visits from my friends from high school, I just wanted it to be special for him. We didn't have much, but we made the most of it all. I remember I bawled that day. I had done it; I made it for a whole year. To me, that was huge because it had been one of the hardest years of my life and the most exhausting. I experienced sleepless nights and days of just wanting to take a shower. Getting out of the door was a major production, but I placed his needs first; it was all worth it. I didn't know what I was doing or how I was doing it, but the truth is that I was doing it.

Isaac was and still is an angel. He never threw a tantrum, and I have absolutely no horrible memories with him. It was almost like he knew we were in this together.

I am forever grateful for all of the nights alone with him. They taught me a lot about relying on myself. Having people around was great but never permanent; Isaac was forever.

The

Purpose

I DECIDED TO

live

IN PURPOSE,

on purpose.

Kailyn Lowry

There are times when purpose does not reveal itself. In those moments, we are forced to just live. We are called to just exist. To find yourself lost is probably the most uncomfortable position, but it is a part of life that we can't avoid, nor should we try. In these moments, we discover what we are made of, and in these moments, we are introduced to the person we will become.

I was so lost for a very long time, much longer than I'd like to admit, but this was my truth. Even though I realized that I was in a relationship that was not going to last, I knew that I still had a purpose that was bigger than anything that I had accomplished. I believe that being lost is a part of the many cycles that we experience in life. It does not matter what phase we are in, or whether we know our purpose, or if we are still in search of it, remember that there is always room for improvement. I knew that I could be and do more.

My decision to return to work when Isaac was five months old was not an easy choice, but doing so restored my belief in myself. After watching all of my friends go off to college, I had lost my self-esteem and so much of who I was. I was the only one who had remained home and who had become a mom. I discovered my power after deciding to work hard for a change. I was desperate for something different to manifest in my life. I knew that if I worked hard enough, I could transcend my current circumstances.

Nothing about that phase of my life was easy, but I did feel like I gained a sense of control that I had once lost. I was making plans to live my life according to my own terms, and for the first time in a while, it felt good. I'd be lying if I said that I was completely happy because I wasn't, but I was working towards something for Isaac and me. Doors of opportunity would soon open.

The

Poetic

Justice

In the end,

I WANT TO BE THE

example,

NOT THE ADVICE.

Kailyn Lowry

The reality of Isaac not having two parents broke my heart, but over time, I recognized that I underestimated how phenomenal he was. Even though Jo and I weren't together, we would be able to provide Isaac with so much love.

Isaac is very smart and far more intuitive than I give him credit for being. Despite all the things I've put him through, he has excelled in school. I underestimated the fight that was embedded inside of him. Isaac likes things to be a certain way; he reminds me so much of myself when I was a kid.

Not too long ago, I asked Isaac if he had to teach his brothers one thing about life, what would it be? He said, "I would teach them how to be patient." He also told me that, "If you're in a line and you rush through people, then they'll keep sending you back, and it'll take a longer time to move forward." Isaac also says he wants to teach his brothers how to do their letters so they can spend less time in Pre-K.

I asked Isaac if he wanted to tell his brothers anything now that would help them when they were older and are able to read this book. He told me that he wants to tell them to respect me more because they don't do it right now. Part of me is laughing, and the other part is glad he's aware. I think all moms can relate when I say that sometimes I feel like I give so much of myself and don't even get a thank you or respect in return. We are working on it in our house.

Isaac said something so impactful the other day. He said, "Lux is one of the greatest babies and deserves to be here. We just earned him, you know?" I don't know what that means, but it might be one of the cutest things I've ever heard.

A

Letter

of Love

to Isaac

Happiness

IS SEEING YOU

smile.

Kailyn Lowry

y first, my baby, the new purpose of my life is you. I didn't know what was going to happen when you entered my life, but I was damn sure going to figure it out. We'd figure it out together. I had never had a real family home, but you must know that your dad and I really did try to give that to you. We tried pretty damn hard given our circumstances and how young we were.

I had no real direction prior to getting pregnant with you, but it never mattered. I was dedicated to making sure that you had the very best of what I could offer. My mom signed off her custody of me like it was no big deal. I was lucky that your dad had parents that had been through this and who eventually took me under their wings. I knew that your dad and I would figure things out, and we have.

The story that you might one day see depicted on the television show is very different in reality. There were times that things didn't go according to plan. There were moments when I felt like the only person that I could count on to be true was the baby growing inside of my stomach - you. The only thing that I have ever been certain of was that I was going to figure this out on my own, at whatever cost. Your dad wasn't perfect. I wasn't perfect, nor will I ever profess to be.

We both experienced the pain of knowing that we loved each other in a way no one else would understand. We shared a permanent bond in you; however, the consistent exhaustion, no sense of direction, and having little to no money, took a toll on our relationship. We never had the ability to experience graduating and going off to college the way the rest of our friends did. This prompted a different reaction in us. Whatever time we got to ourselves, we didn't necessarily want to spend it together.

This is a part of the process when you attempt to love. There is always a possibility that love won't last, but the most important thing to remember is that it existed. You were thought of and conceived in love. There is nothing that can ever separate the bond that we have managed to forge. You meant the world to me when you were born, and you mean the world to me as I watch you grow. If I've never told you before, I live because of you. You saved me, and I will be eternally grateful for you.

A Moment in Time

Isaac,

You turn eight in nine short days. Some days I look at you in awe because I'm so proud of you, and I cannot believe I've gotten to spend the last eight years with you. Where did the time go? I don't think anyone can really appreciate that question until she has kids of her own. I was over-joyed when you got off the bus today and said you had practiced basketball and had enjoyed a good day at school. You did your homework, and then we had your favorite tacos for dinner. I feel like that's all we ever eat! One of my favorite things that we do is sing our hearts out to Sam Smith in the car. We sang all the way to your dad's house. I just want to thank you for a day like today that makes all the hard and exhausting days so worth it. I love you!

Mom

FOUR

Lincoln

AND EVEN WHEN I'VE

given you

ALL OF MY LOVE,

LET ME LOVE YOU A

little more.

—❤—

Kailyn Lowry

The

Birth

of

Lincoln

THE BRIGHTNESS

in your eyes

LETS ME KNOW

THAT I AM

loved.

Kailyn Lowry

inc's birth story was a little different. I was extremely pregnant, and slightly overdue. Linc was stubborn and refused to be born on anyone else's time. Weird, he's still like that today! I was rooting for the due date to be 11-12-13 because it was cool, but when it came and went, I swear I was over it. I can remember going to a football game with some friends and having a good time. It was a memorable night with a full moon when Javi and I remembered that we hadn't picked any names for girl babies. If Linc had turned out to be a girl, we would have been so screwed. After the game, we returned home and went to bed, but about two hours later, I felt the contractions. It was in the middle of the night when I went into labor, and I also had to be concerned about Isaac. I was thankful for Javi's mom who lived with us; she was able to stay with Isaac. Javi and I headed to the hospital, and because it was just us, it was nice.

To my surprise, the difference between Isaac's birth and the birth of Linc was night and day. Javi was very quiet for me and patient with me. I used the labor ball a lot and really just waited. This was the first baby in the Marroquin family, so I think there was a lot of built up anticipation for the baby. The question of the day was whether or not it would be a boy or a girl. After sixteen hours and a fairly quiet and peaceful delivery, Lincoln Marshall was born. I laugh to this day when Javi talks about how "it was nothing like the movies". I feel proud because I did a good job with Linc's labor and his delivery!

Lincoln and I had an amazing bond. He was almost always by my side for the first year of his life. Linc loved nursing, and he did nurse at all times day after day. Nursing him was more difficult and tiring than it had been with my other boys, but Linc was a tiny terror who won my heart. Lincoln taught me a lot of patience, and Lord knows, as a mom of boys, you need patience.

The

Passion

DO IT WITH

passion

OR NOT AT ALL.

Kailyn Lowry

All I knew was that I wanted so desperately to be a part of a real family again. I wanted Isaac to have the life that I could have only wished I had. I was driven and motivated by the prospect of this wish becoming a reality, and along came Javi. I believed with my heart that we would spend the rest of our lives together, and we resolved to do just that. With love and family as our motivation, it became us against the world. With a baby on the way, there was nothing that could stop us, or so we thought.

Prior to Linc's birth, I struggled so hard with the fact that I was about to have another child. I never thought that I could love another person as much as I loved Isaac. I didn't believe that I had the capacity to love the same way. I was so afraid that I couldn't be the mother to Linc that I was to Isaac. I had always wanted siblings for Isaac, and there was a part of me that was so excited. For whatever reason, when reality manifested itself, I didn't know if I could do it. I quickly learned that love multiplies, it doesn't divide. The passion that I had locked away in my heart was now thriving and served as the only persuasion I needed to keep love alive.

The

Pain

YOU CAN EITHER

BE DRIVEN BY THE

shock

OF WHAT

could happen

OR THE HURT FROM

WHAT MIGHT NEVER

become.

Kailyn Lowry

ruth moment: I knew going into the marriage with Javi that I would regret it. We were fighting constantly and not even sleeping in the same bed. I was overcome and filled with doubt at all times. I was trying to convince myself that things would get better in time, but they never did. The reality was that I had been in search of a lie, and it wasn't because we didn't love each other. I would venture to say that it was because it was never meant to be. There are times in life that you don't get to have what you want, even when you think that you deserve it. I was in search of happiness, but I kept coming up short. Even as I wrote my book, *Pride Over Pity*, I lied. I wrote about how happy I was in my marriage to Javi. It was all a ditch attempt to try to convince myself. Of all the people watching our lives unfold, I now realize that while we were convincing the world, I was the one that needed to be convinced that love was real and that happiness would find me.

While searching for love with Javi, I was taking classes here and there and still managing to work two jobs. One job was at the mall, and the other was at a dog grooming salon. Real life as a mother and as a wife was in full swing. Even though everything was in motion, I was still very lost and very confused. The only thing that I knew was that I owed it to Isaac and now to Linc to give them a family. Neither Javi nor I quite knew what we were doing, but we did know that we were committed to something greater than ourselves, the kids.

The

Power

I AM CONVINCED

THAT THE

only

WAY TO HAVE

power

IS TO TAKE IT.

Kailyn Lowry

*P*atterns of love that are destructive can only last for so long. The pieces of the puzzle were not fitting for Javi and me. He told me on several occasions that he had filed for a divorce. I never knew if he had really done so or not. I was afraid in so many ways. I was afraid to start over, afraid to fail at love again, and afraid to be the mother of two children from two different relationships that didn't work.

Eventually, I got sick and tired of being sick and tired, and I went to visit an attorney to find out what I could about a divorce. I had never been through one, and I had so many questions. Would I be able to find a new home for the boys and me? Would I be okay on my own? Fear had me bound; I didn't go through with it.

I made the decision to step outside of my comfort zone and to denounce fear just before Javi was deployed for the military.

Around that same time, there were tons of rumors that I was with someone else. Regardless of what the public opinion was, I had not dated anyone else until after I officially filed for a divorce from Javi. Even though I had friends at the house, I was never with a guy alone. It was all B.S. When Javi accused me of cheating on the show, I didn't defend myself. I never cheated on Javi. I was just done. I was going to take my life back and begin to live for the boys and me.

The

Purpose

THE ONLY WAY TO

love who you are

IS TO NOT

hate the moments

IN LIFE THAT

shaped you.

Kailyn Lowry

There are times when the merry-go-round won't stop turning to let you off. In those moments, you have to ride with the emotion and momentum until the cycle stops. When I was close to the end of my pregnancy with Linc, I cried all the time. I was so anxious, and I would get upset about everything. I worried all the time. When Javi would take Isaac to his dad to give me a minute to catch my breath, I would worry that something would happen to them on the way. I now know that my anxiety stemmed from my wondering if I would have enough love to go around with a new baby on the way. How can I love another child the way that I love Isaac? He was my whole world. I even told Javi that maybe he should just take the new baby, and I would go off with Isaac. I could not believe that these were the thoughts that I was having, but they were real. From the outside looking in, this wasn't logical. I was married, and my husband had a good job. We had cars. What could have been so wrong? Everything! You can't live a lie forever. Eventually, the truth will make itself known, and the truth was that Javi and I were not going to make it.

After giving birth to Lincoln, I cried so hard. When I saw him, it was instant love! I had no idea that I would be able to love him like I loved Isaac. I had no idea that my love for both of them would multiply. In that moment, I knew that I could do it. I knew that I could be a mom of two boys. Through it all, my kids have proven to me in so many ways that my purpose is to be a mom. It is the greatest joy of my life.

The

Poetic

Justice

WE MUST DO MORE THAN

just live.

WE MUST ALSO

discover love,

AND IN THE PROCESS,

discover ourselves.

Kailyn Lowry

We should never settle for anything. We shouldn't settle for a love that won't last. We shouldn't settle for a relationship that won't work, and we shouldn't settle for less than what we know we deserve. This is still something that I am working on, but I know it to be true.

I've managed to assume a great deal of guilt for bringing Linc into a marriage that did not work. Like Isaac, I wanted him to have a family with two loving parents living together. I could not do this if both Javi and I were settling.

Through it all, I have learned that it is far worse to teach your children to stay in an unhappy relationship than it is to actually leave one that is not destined for success. I never wanted to be the example of an unhealthy marriage that they didn't need to see. Nothing is worth compromising your happiness. This revelation taught me that I was not only settling in my marriage but also with my personal goals. I knew that I was meant to do more. I was longing for school and to better myself. I knew that when I put my mind to it, I could be something. I had my foot in the door for television, radio, and film endeavors, and I had resolved that even if I did not make it in front of the camera, I could find success behind it. When Lincoln was a little under a year old, I enrolled in school at Delaware State for Mass Communications.

When I enrolled, I was nervous because I was nursing Lincoln exclusively. I didn't know if I would fit in because I was not the traditional student. Unlike my classmates, I wasn't living on campus, and I had kids. I was angry because I felt like Javi didn't want me to go back to school, but I was also thankful because his mom was willing to help watch the baby.

It felt good to know that I was working toward something that I wanted to do to become the best version of myself.

I asked Lincoln the same question. "Is there anything you want to say to your brothers for mommy's book?" He said, "I want to tell them that they are my best friends." He also added that he likes his family and mac and cheese.

When I asked the boys what their thoughts were about having Lux added to the family, Linc said, "I love him."

I couldn't have said it better myself.

A
Letter
of Love
To Lincoln

THE MOMENT

YOU THINK YOU

know love,

A SMALL REMINDER

IS SENT TO GROW

your heart

EVEN BIGGER.

Kailyn Lowry

It's hard for me to find the right words to say to you. From an outsider's perspective, things were perfect, and it seemed that I did things the right way with you. I have to disagree because I feel like my relationship and marriage were rushed and under extreme pressure. I think things would have been completely different if we didn't have the pressure of all of our viewers from the show and from so many outside opinions. Reality television is a very strange thing to be a part of, especially in the way that we are involved. Our family's demise was caught between the editing to make the shows make sense to the viewers and the paychecks that we were hard pressed to get. I look at you, and I look at Isaac, and I wish I could have made it work for you. I wish we could all be together in one house at all times. When I look at Lux, I cannot imagine our lives without him. It's just one of those things that even I can't explain. What I can explain is the fullness of my love for you. You awakened a compartment in my heart that I never knew existed. Only you could do that, and as much as I love you, I am not alone. You are loved by so many.

You have an amazing family on your dad's side. You've lived with your dad, grandparents, and godmother/aunt for almost all of your life. What could be better? I have so much love for your family. I'll admit that at times life can be frustrating. It's hard co-parenting with your dad and grandparents, but I am thankful that everyone wants the best for you. Grandparents are always the pushovers, and when grandkids are around them, they can get away with everything. Your grandparents are no different. I feel that I am seen as the mean one, the disciplinarian. I'm the one who is at home and sets exact times for routine things. I'm the one who tries to get you to eat healthy foods and not all of the fun stuff. You will learn that moms are this way.

Sometimes, I feel as if I'll never be good enough for you because you've got so much when you are with your dad. I just want the best for you; we all do. Moreover, I want you to grow up with discipline, drive, and a true understanding of boundaries and rules. I never want to fail you as a parent in that regard.

When you were much younger, you couldn't be without your dad or me. Today, you are so independent, and at times, it hurts. I just want you to know how much I love you. I don't ever want you to feel the need to choose one family over another. I have always been here, and I will always be here.

You have such a huge personality packaged in a pint sized kid. I waited so long for you to speak when you were a baby. After the age of two, and in true Linc fashion, you spoke when you were ready. I didn't know what I was doing wrong, but out of nowhere you started talking with an attitude like no other. You are sweet and caring, even when you don't get your way. This says a lot about how amazing you are. I can always count on you to tell it like it is. You understand when you are wrong, and you always express compassion and empathy for others. Even though I've called you a sour patch kid, you are the sweetest love I know.

Mom

A Moment in Time

JANUARY 9, 2018

I watch Lincoln in amazement almost every day. His imagination and goofiness are inspiring. His love for life makes me so happy. I hope he never loses sight of his brighter side. I laugh so much with him. People ask what his name is all the time, because he goes from Lincoln to a superhero at least once a day. I'm so proud of him. He always tells the truth and acknowledges when he's wrong. He genuinely loves people and sees the good in everyone. It's amazing to see the kind of person he is at just four years old.

Last year his teacher even told us that he was the perfect kid. Lincoln is the example she uses in her classroom. I think I cried that day!

FIVE

Lux

THE PRESENCE OF

new life

IS A PRESENT.

Kailyn Lowry

The

Birth

of

Lux

If there's anything that hurts more than a miscarriage, it's a second one. When you've had multiple miscarriages, you feel excitement and then heartbreak. After multiple miscarriages and being told that I might not be able to have more kids, I was feeling conflicted. Once the option was almost taken from me, I knew that I absolutely wanted more kids. A friend once told me, "If you've thought about having another child, you won't regret having that child, but if you've thought about it and never gave birth, you could live to regret it."

When I found out that I was pregnant, I was 10000% sure that I wanted this baby. I wasn't so sure if the universe was conspiring with me. Every single day I woke up wondering if I would see blood when I went to the bathroom. This was going to be my third baby, and I felt like I should have known that every pregnancy is different. I also believed that not every small thing needed a call to the doctor. I just wanted to be extremely careful. I knew that my prior miscarriages weren't my fault, but I felt that if I were be super careful this time, I could prevent another miscarriage. I was not going to let it happen again because I would call the doctor every time I had a weird feeling. The doctor would probably hate me, but that would be fine. Until I was seventeen weeks pregnant, I distinctly remember that I was still checking for blood every time I went to the bathroom. This baby was coming home with me.

As I prepared to become a mother of three, I didn't question whether or not my heart had the capacity to love another little human being. I would have to say that my pregnancy with Lux was the most vulnerable time of my life. I questioned myself and didn't understand what a future with his father would become. I must admit it, my boys were there with me through everything. They were both physically and emotionally supportive. I believe that there is just something very special about being a mother of boys.

My water broke at one thirty in the morning. I thought that I would be able to shower and take a nap before going to the hospital. My friend, Rachel, was at home with me, so she called the doctor who advised me to go immediately to the hospital. At first I was going to have Chris meet me there, but I was hesitant. We had not spoken or had any contact for two weeks prior to this time; therefore, I was nervous just to call him. I called anyway and Chris did come to the house to get me. When we were about halfway to the hospital, I felt an urge that was almost too much to bear. Before I knew it, I yelled out, "Chris, I have to push." I was holding onto his arm as tightly as I could. I don't think that my nails could have gone any deeper into his arm. I barely made it into the hospital bed, and the staff did their best to get my IV's started. I tried to tell the nurses that I had to push because I was dilating fast. I could feel it. "I have to push! I have to push!" I could not say it enough. The baby was coming. As the nurse was checking me, I went from eight to ten centimeters in her hands. Chris told me that as I started to push again, everyone went into panic mode. It became necessary for the nurse to hit the emergency button to call for all of the nurses to come and assist. As they all ran into my room, I noticed that my doctor never made it.

I had begged for an epidural, but I never got it because there wasn't enough time. My baby boy, Lux, was born at three a.m., the entire labor and delivery lasted for one hour and thirty minutes.

This was Chris' first baby. It felt like everything around us was moving so fast, but it seemed as if Chris and I were stopped in time. After they placed this little baby on my chest, I asked, "Are you guys going to tell me what it is?"

I thought I had a girl. The baby had so much hair. "It's a boy!" I don't even remember who said it. After that, Chris never left my side. He stayed with me every single day in the hospital.

After we left the hospital, he came to the house and stayed with us as well. We tried to get back together and work things out, but it only lasted for about a month. After that brief time of being together, we didn't speak for a period of eight months.

The

Passion

LIVING LIFE WITHOUT

passion

IS NOT LIVING AT ALL.

Kailyn Lowry

hris and I started off having so much fun together. There were no strings attached; we shared good energy, and lots of laughs. I think I was attracted to the fact that Chris didn't want anything to do with television or the media. He brought me back to a place where I didn't have to fit a storyline or a fictitious character that was made up for me. I could runaway with him and just be myself. Things were fine that way, and we fell for each other as we spent more time together. As time evolved, so did the strings. I didn't want to share him with anyone else, and I was made to believe that I wasn't sharing him. Eventually, I would find out otherwise.

Although the passion between Chris and me peaked my attention, I would discover that the passion for my boys would sustain me. I must admit that being a single mother is one of the most exhausting things I've ever been through. It's exhausting emotionally and physically, and a lot of time is spent wondering if you're doing enough to make sure your children have everything they need.

Nobody really talks about the unwavering bond that is created between you and your children and the bond that is created between the siblings. I look at my life today, and I would never put anyone or anything above my children. Right now, nobody else is worthy of my time. I pour myself into my kids, and caring for them is now the way that I define passion.

The

Pain

THE MOMENT I HIT

rock bottom,

I BEGAN THE

CONSTRUCTION OF A

new life.

—♥—

Kailyn Lowry

here do I begin? I've experienced a plateau of pain that I've denied to myself and to others. As a coping mechanism, I've hidden my feelings in so many places that I often can't remember where they are. The one place that I couldn't hide my true emotions was in my journal. I wrote about the truth, the pain, and the moments of what felt like agony in my journal because it was safe. Making them public for the first time is scary, but telling the truth is what will set me free. So, here goes...

September 20, 2017

I lost a toxic relationship, and Chris lost spending every day with our son.

Now the baby sleeps on Chris's side of the bed just like he did when I was pregnant.

Because I am capable of doing this on my own, doesn't mean that I should. Lux has two parents, but I find myself alone as a party of one.

October 8, 2017

As I reflect over all that has happened, I realize that in the first six weeks of Lux being here, I've been hurt in so many ways. I've had my bedroom window broken while the baby was asleep with me in the room. My back door had been broken while all of my kids were at home, and I've had shit about me told to my children. I don't care if the baby is six weeks or six years old, a dad should not talk down about the mother of his child.

Let's talk about finances. I've been left to take care of everything. Even the responsibility for all of the baby formula was left up to me. I kind of knew that this would be a possibility, but I guess I just wanted to be proved wrong. Is it too much to ask if the baby needs anything? Whether we were on good or bad terms, Chris could have at least asked if I needed help. Because I can be totally responsible for our child doesn't mean that I should take care of everything. I'm so glad that my child has so many other people in his corner. There's so much to the story that so many people don't know. It's depressing because it's clear that everyone is frustrated with me, but no one can really see my viewpoint in this situation. I don't get it.

I didn't wake up one morning and decide that I was going to cut Chris out of our lives. There are reasons why I feel the way that I do. Just because he has a biological connection to the baby, doesn't mean he's best for the baby. I do all of the hard work; I'm up with him at all hours of the night. I'm bringing him everywhere I go. Why should I give up my holidays or other milestones with our child? I shouldn't because I take on all of the responsibilities; therefore, I feel like I should get all of the rewards.

October 21, 2017

Lux doesn't have his dad in the same way the other boys do, and I am sorry for that. I loved his dad, but he caused me so much pain. I feel badly about the choice I made for his father, but I also have to thank him for giving me one of my greatest joys–Lux.

January 6, 2018

This past weekend, we went to our good friend's birthday party. It was a party for Isaac's best friend. They have been best friends since we moved here to Delaware. They've been like family to us. The party was crowded, and they had many activities for the children. I can't complain at all because my kids were exceptionally well behaved that day. They didn't fight or cry with each other or with the other kids. I noticed Lux sitting up by himself for extended periods of time. We were getting ready to leave, and like all the other days, I was preparing the kids for the ride home. I was struggling with the car seat while trying to help the other two get their coats on. For whatever reason, I don't know why, I just got so emotional. I couldn't get out of the house and into the car fast enough. I don't even think we said goodbye to everyone.

In the moment, I was feeling overwhelmed, and I didn't want anyone to see me that way. Luckily, before we got to the car, and before the tears fell from my eyes, our friend's mom stopped us and said, "Hey Kail, I got this gift for the boys to share. It's not much, but it's just a little something I thought you'd like." I thanked her so much because it was thoughtful. She hugged me and said, "I'm so proud of you." I couldn't say anything. I already didn't know what I was feeling. After I got the kids into the car, I completely lost it.

Motherhood is such a rollercoaster of emotions. I was so happy our friend's son had just turned one, and that we could be there to celebrate. I was even happier that my kids made getting there and being there easy for me. For every bit of happiness that I felt, I was equally sad. By the time I got home, I was completely fine. I don't think I could have prepared myself for the loneliness that can accompany single parenthood.

I know I can't be in a relationship right now, and I don't want to be, but that doesn't make it any easier on some days.

The

Power

The Truth

THAT MIGHT MAKE SOME

angry

IS THE SAME TRUTH

THAT WILL SET YOU

free.

♡

Kailyn Lowry

ruth Moment: I don't think I ever felt powerful when I was pregnant with Lux. I have to take full accountability. I was not making good choices. I knew that Chris and I were not in a position to have a baby. It makes sense to me that I was emotionally drained during the pregnancy because I was in a relationship that was not healthy. I don't think I could have felt powerful then. I was so vulnerable and desperate. I was so insecure about so many things.

There was a period of time when the relationship was on and off again, and I was constantly questioning my worth. I had to come to terms with the fact that I had three kids by three different men. What hurts even worse was that the one that I wanted, didn't want me. He was out being with other people and not looking for a real relationship. I was spending time questioning why I was not good enough. I was also upset because I felt that no one else would want me. All of my relationships had ended the same way. Even today, I am struggling with the effects of that relationship. I have, however, discovered power in speaking this truth. Sometimes the most powerful thing that we can do is walk in unfiltered truth. This is mine.

The

Purpose

LIFE SEEMS SO

random

UNTIL YOU REALIZE

THAT IT WAS ALL

meant to be.

Kailyn Lowry

As a mother, my purpose was rooted solely in raising my children, until I realized that I was born to fill many different roles that would allow me to exemplify strength, creativity, and the gumption to push the limits to care for our family. I had skills that exceeded the walls of my home, and I was determined to use them for our greater good.

December 8, 2017

They say it takes a village to raise a child, but I never fully understood that until now. During Lux's first year of life, I had a core group of friends who would do anything for him and for his brothers. Nothing I can do will ever express my gratitude. There are times that I worry that I spread myself too thin trying to do too many things while balancing motherhood in a good and healthy way. I've learned that there are other things outside of motherhood that I need to do to "fill my cup" to provide an income to support us. This has become my drive and also my determination to ensure that we have all that we need to live, be happy, and thrive.

June 14, 2018

I recently returned from Europe where I had traveled while the kids were with their dads. The whole time I was there, I couldn't help but think about how I wanted my kids to experience these new cultures that I had witnessed. As much as I want to travel with my kids, I haven't really put too much effort into it aside from our yearly family vacations. My kids have no idea how blessed we are financially at the cost of my privacy and humility. Of course, it's for them. I don't want them to be spoiled in that way. I want them to be spoiled with culture and experiences and to know that there is life outside our hometown of Dover, Delaware.

My kids don't know any life different from the life they have now. I'm afraid that this is going to set them up for failure. They don't understand the concept of working in order to obtain what they need or want. I'm working on this as a parent.

The

Poetic

Justice

ONLY

broken hearts

OPEN.

❤

Kailyn Lowry

When I was young, I made the mistake of trying so hard to find love, but it all crumbled. In the process, my kids got attached and met people that they didn't necessarily need to meet. I know better now. That's poetic justice.

November 24, 2017

Part of me is thankful that everything with Lux has happened while he is a baby. This means that he won't see my struggle with his father. Part of me wishes I could let him experience it on his own and make the decision himself. Either way it goes, he deserves better. Lux, you deserve the world.

November 27, 2017

I've struggled with whether or not to include Lux's dad's family in his life while his dad is not in it. Some people would agree that it's best to let his family be a part of his life. Maybe it would encourage his dad to become involved, but it's not that easy. I never wanted him to not be included; I wanted the exact opposite. Things have just gotten so bad that this is the way it needed to happen. I had to have a legal agreement put in place, so that I no longer allowed my personal feelings to get in the way. Lux's relationship with his father should be all his own, but what does that mean if he is not present? There were so many times that I wanted to just say "no" to allowing them access to you, but after a short time, I realized that it doesn't matter what I think. It doesn't matter what Lux's father and I think of each other as long as we have his best interest in mind and at heart. As much as it hurts, I realize that I have to give Lux the opportunity to develop his own relationship with his family and make decisions such as this for himself, with no judgment from me.

A

Letter

of Love

to Lux

And sometimes,

I FEEL THE NEED TO

love you

A LITTLE BIT MORE.

Kailyn Lowry

As I write this letter, you are turning four months old before my very eyes. It seems like all your "firsts" are coming at once. You're reaching for toys and objects in front of you. You belly laugh so hard I want to cry with happiness. There is something about a baby really laughing for the first time that would make anyone's heart melt. You grab your feet with your hands, and it's the cutest thing ever. You're also trying to sit up by yourself. It's you, Lux. There's just something so special about you and knowing that you're my baby. You're probably going to be my last baby, and I'm so thankful for you. I'm thankful that I am in a place where I can spend all of this time with you. I know that this time will fly by, and so I bask in the moments.

Nothing about our lives is ideal, except the white picket fence outside. Since I had your brother, Isaac, remaining on television has presented quite a unique dynamic for our lives. I'm thankful, but sometimes I am regretful. Overall, I am thankful for the opportunities. However, being in the public eye allows for opinions and judgement from people who don't affect our family. The media sometimes twists things, or makes things more dramatic than they truly are. I'm sure you will wonder why I say that and what it all has to do with you? The truth is that I want you to be prepared. You may hear things about me or your dad, or you may hear things about your family and life in general that may not always be true. This is my attempt to set the record straight for you. It is my hope that you understand my point of view and how hard some decisions have been.

The first two months after your arrival, I struggled emotionally. I didn't mind getting up at all hours of the night. I didn't mind getting your brothers off to school, sports, and picking them up, nor did I mind running errands and timing everything around your feedings and naps. I recognized and appreciated that this is what moms do. What I struggled with was doing everything alone. I really wanted to share these experiences with your dad. I fell in love with something about him, and I wanted us to be in love, together, loving you. For the first few months, you and I co-slept, and it was nice to have those cuddles. When you were about three months old, you started to sleep in your room, and I went to bed alone. You were here, but I was alone.

Things have been emotional and a little chaotic over the years, but I will say that this whole situation has proved to me that with you and your brothers, we are going to get through everything that we face. We aren't going to judge each other's mistakes, because those mistakes don't define us. I really just want you to be happy and to work hard at whatever it is you need to do. Believe me when I say that the easy way isn't always the best way.

You've reminded me to embrace the crazy that is our lives. It's okay that our house is a little messy sometimes. We stay on the move with all the sports, pick ups, and drop offs between the three of you. There was one time that your brother had to wear his soccer cleats to baseball practice because we had no time to change. It's okay that you've had six "blow-outs" in one day, and now I'm putting one of your brother's pull ups on you until we make it home safely. This is our new normal. I just want you, Isaac, and Lincoln to know that, whatever it is, I'm going to come through with it. I'm going to make it work for all of you.

While your dad and I don't see eye to eye, I know that he will come through in some capacity for you. He's graduating, and through everything, both of your parents are college graduates! That wasn't easy. Although we both exceeded the standard four year college plan, we still made it happen. I know for a fact that graduating from college was something your dad wanted for himself, but he also wanted it for you. You are the child of two college graduates.

Seeing your face sparks so many emotions that I often find them hard to contain. They hit me out of nowhere. The four of us could be having a good day, a busy day, and I will suddenly look around me and realize that I couldn't give you and your brothers what you deserve. More than anything, you deserve both parents, together in one house. It pains me even further to realize that I couldn't, at the very minimum, give you two parents that could get along. I wanted so desperately to have you witness your parents communicate respectfully and civilly for you. I am still hopeful that one day this will be our reality.

In the meantime, I will keep being inspired to grow as a person and as a mother. I will continue to be the example that you need and deserve. You are a constant reminder to me to never be complacent or to get too comfortable. Today, I am officially in "beast mode". I am always looking for the next project or job that can sustain us and help me to walk in purpose. I want you guys to be able to have everything, but I also want you all to know the value of a dollar and what it means to keep moving and working hard for the things you want and need. I have said all of this to say that no matter who comes and goes, you will always be able to count on me, or should I say "us". We've formed quite the family. It's Mom, Isaac, Lincoln, and you. We all love you, Lux!

A NOTE FROM
Isaac & Lincoln

Isaac – I love you. You are the best. We will spend time with you every day. We're glad we have you here. You'll have the best life ever.

Lincoln – Lux, you are the best baby in the whole world. I will play with you whenever you want to play. You will always be "Baby Lo".

SIX

Dear

Kailyn

*L*ife is going to kick your ass. Some moments will be a result of the cards that you have been dealt and others a result of the choices that you will make. No matter what, you will be responsible for picking up the pieces and assembling a picture of the life that you wish to see manifested.

You will not have countless examples of love to serve as a point of reference. As much as it hurts you, you will not meet your father until the age of eighteen. Allow me to warn you that your opportunities to spend time with him will be scarce.

Defining love will prove to be challenging. Just remember you will feel it in your heart. Even when you feel rejected, never forget that true love will always find you. You will demonstrate love in ways that you can't imagine through the children that you will give life. They will become your greatest joy and teach you to see yourself and the world differently.

Your most challenging conquest will not be in giving love but instead in discovering how to truly love yourself. Your experiences will force you to question who you are and what you believe. You will have to go through the fire, but in the end, you will discover that it has been within you all the while.

Learn not to shy from change and what feels like turbulent times. Transition will become your greatest form of evolution. As much as you will be led to believe that you are responsible for having all of the answers, the universe has your best interest in mind.

When you feel hopeless, stay the course. Step outside of your comfort zone. Just on the other side of fear is a new found life of opportunities and adventures.

Sincerely,
In Search of Love

SEVEN

A

Letter

of

Love

ear Boys,

Every single day, I think and say to myself, "I really have three kids...three boys." I laugh to myself when I see your faces. You have molded me into a person who recognizes that love conquers all.

I must admit that teaching you how to align the dishes in the dishwasher is a lot harder than I thought. Even so, what you are doing now will likely follow you throughout your lives. You often argue about who's doing which chores and absolutely do not follow the chore chart that I made on the fridge. Such is life.

Lincoln and Isaac, you are both so good with Lux. Both of you have been helpful with entertaining him while I get things done around the house or steal a few extra minutes in the shower.

Lux, you think your brothers are so funny.

Lincoln, you always go with the flow which is very much like me. It's almost like nothing phases you, but if something does bother you, you aren't afraid to say it. I love that about you. It's a pretty amazing characteristic.

Isaac, you are me as a child. I see so much of myself in you. I know you try to go with the flow, but ultimately you want things done your way. You have a fire inside of you and nothing goes without being questioned. It's a blessing and a curse. You're so smart and intuitive, and sometimes I forget that you're only eight years old. When you discover something you like, you will research and explore it with a passion. I know this ambition will take you very far in life; however, there is one thing I need you to know. Everything in life will not come to you as easily as what you learn in school. You will not excel in every single thing you do. You will have to work harder at some things, and some things will require more patience. You will be an achiever, and you will find great pleasure in knowing what you have finally accomplished.

Linc, I thought you were the wild one, but now I'm seeing how much Lux gets into everything. It amazes me how smart you are and how you figure things out. You are so curious and fearless but also cautious. I can tell that you really think through the decisions that you make. If something doesn't feel right, you won't take the risk. That will be an amazing quality as you get older. Knowing how to trust your instincts is important.

It is possible that you will hear a lot about me from the perspectives of others. I want you to remember that so much is easier said than done. If nothing else, I want to open your hearts to see things for yourselves and to change your perspective on love. I want your hearts to be opened to love always. I made huge mistakes and didn't really gain perspective until it was too late. If I can teach you anything, it is to love yourselves first and foremost. I also urge you to love and trust each other. Doing so will mean that you won't be forced to look for it in other places. Love should enhance what you already have and know; however, it should not be the only focus of your search.

At first, you will never be able to know a person's true intentions. Be honest even though it may be incredibly hard. Be honest with yourself and be honest with those around you. Be honest with friends and those who are not close to you. I'm not advising you to go out of your way to tell someone what is wrong or that you don't like a chosen outfit. In the end, those things won't be important. I am saying that you must learn to be honest about your feelings and your intentions. Doing so will ensure that no one will be able to question you, your morals, or your convictions. Defend your loved one's names when someone speaks negatively of them. It may not make sense now, but it will come full circle.

DO NOT retaliate. Karma is real, and she doesn't need your help. If someone does mistreat you, I promise you that it has nothing to do with you.

All of these things sound so cliché, but they are real life lessons that are rooted in truth and in love. If you're genuine and honest from the very beginning, you will understand much sooner. I heard that your heart doesn't only belong to you. All the people you encounter will feel a little piece of you, so even on your bad days, be the best you can to people.

Read and travel. It sounds weird, but educating yourselves on so many different things from what you read and the places that you can explore is life changing. You will not only learn about other cultures, but you will learn about yourself. You will become well rounded when you realize that there is more to life than what's directly in front of you.

I leave you with these lessons for your future:

Relationships

are

very hard.

ocial media and television will add challenges and temptation as well as the opinions of others into the relationship. Don't let that influence you. Do what you feel is right by your family and you and not by what you think people want to see or what they think you should do.

Love

your

brothers.

This may be a selfish one, but nothing makes my day more than when I see you and your brothers playing and loving each other. I never had siblings and would have loved to have had them, appreciate them, be kind to them, and love them. Love your brothers unconditionally.

Work

hard.

ou may not always be happy right where you are at a specific time or place but stay busy and work hard to move forward. It'll be frustrating, and you'll lose your patience and cry, but if you "bust your butt" a bit more, you will get to the next step wherever that might be for you. Do not remain stagnant.

Accept responsibility for your actions.

*E*verybody messes up. You will make mistakes, and that's okay. Accept your imperfections and move forward. The hard part that I've learned about this is that sometimes you don't even realize that you've made a mistake until it's all said and done, and you've had time to reflect on it. Hindsight is always 20/20, and that brings me to something that applies in all situations. In relationships, jobs, friendships, and everything that you do, DO NOT IGNORE RED FLAGS, and trust your instincts. Luckily, in our case, I ignored the red flags, but I got you as a result, and I will forever be thankful. Most of the time, when you have a feeling that something isn't right, you are right.

Whatever you resolve to do, do it with love in your hearts. Love is the most powerful sentiment that lives and breathes inside of you.

Mom

CONCLUSION

Dear

World

ear World,
What is love?

I hear people saying all the time that "you can't miss what you've never had", but in my case, nothing could be farther from the truth. I feel like I have missed being loved my entire life. To miss being loved is a pain that I wish upon no one.

It is possible that I don't have what it takes to truly define love. I never took the time to correlate the pain of my past to my present, but with a clearer perspective, it is possible that there are some lines to be drawn. If a girl's father is her first love, and he becomes the point of reference for how she loves, it makes sense that I was aimlessly in search of it. I never knew that kind of love. I had no example to mirror. I had only known what I felt in my relationships. I knew what I liked and what I didn't like, and I knew how love at times hurts. I knew that I desired to be loved in a way that I didn't even know how to recognize.

As much as I'd like to believe that LOVE is just a four letter word, my heart always wants more. I've discovered the greatest fulfillment I've ever known in giving love to my boys, Isaac, Lincoln, and Lux. I was born to be the light of love in their lives, and I will do just that. Today, I stand in truth to right the wrongs and to ensure that my children know the fullness of love for themselves. I will never allow them to feel the emptiness that I have felt. They deserve so much more. Everything that I have done and everything that I will do is to help them discover love.

Today, it is my belief that we are all in search of love. We all desire to be understood by those who love us. Desiring to be loved keeps us in a constant state of transition. We are ever evolving, and evolution is never a bad thing when it is rooted in discovering our purpose and becoming better for those around us. Evolving is never a bad thing when we seek to create good in the world. I am still trying to figure it all out, but the good news is that many of us will cling to the hope that is within us. If you've made mistakes, remember to not be too hard on yourself. When you desire to love and be loved, it makes you get your shit together. It is as simple as that.

So with the fullness of my heart, I can proclaim that love is not only a feeling, it's an action. It is something that we have the capacity in which to grow. We can give it freely, but we must also protect it at all times and recognize that everyone deserves our love, but not everyone deserves our hearts. Love is far more than a four letter word. It is the fuel that serves as the source of energy for our existence. Much like air, we all need love. Never forget that you deserve the love that you dream of having. Most importantly, love will not come to you if you haven't first learned to love yourself. You won't have to search far; the greatest love already lives inside of you.

Afterword

Kail's relationships tell a lot about who she is and how she has grown over the years. So much has changed over time. Growing up without the traditional family model affects people in different ways. Some become what they know, and others search to find something that they've never had. I believe Kail will never stop searching. She has spent the majority of her life giving her kids everything that she never had and trying to create the family that she's always wanted. Even though she didn't necessarily receive the love that she has been in search of, she has found a way to give it to her children each and every day, and that's not easy.

It's been hard for her to understand what love is and how to find it for herself. I believe that some of her relationships have failed because she has not had anything to base them on or to know what she deserves. She's searching for love blindly and trying to create the life that she has dreamt of.

I didn't know her while she was with Jo, but I do know that she was young and in love. From that love an unexpected pregnancy evolved. With Javi, I think she found something that resembled love in her heart. She had discovered a form of love that she didn't have before. Still young, they both tried and gave each other the love they could while battling through many challenges. In the end, there was a lack of a foundation to make it clear that this was not the life she had hoped for. The most significant change that I have witnessed in Kail's ability to love is definitely with Chris. Chris was the first person that Kail has ever truly loved this deeply.

Experiencing love in its fullness like this is overwhelming. With Kail, this love has manifested later in life. She was almost at a point where she believed that loving another person other than her children so powerfully was not possible. Watching her amidst this overpowering emotion towards one person is something she never displayed in all the years I have known her. Love that is this strong can go in either direction and is solely dependent upon whether or not it is reciprocated.

As her friend, I will always be concerned that she receives the love that she so desperately wants to give to others, and a love that she now knows is possible. Seeing Kail actually be in love with someone and giving all of her love and emotion was crazy to witness. These are all feelings we openly discussed that would never happen to her. What makes it so compelling is that she has now realized that she could love all along. A revelation like this can change someone's entire life.

My only hope now is that she will find someone to reciprocate love with. When love, respect, and loyalty are mutual, it is the most amazing feeling. Amidst a love she's never felt before, she is now more vulnerable. Loving in this way makes us all vulnerable, and that's not a bad thing if you are with the right person. For Kail, loving entirely has made her do things that she otherwise wouldn't for someone who wouldn't do that for her. We've all been there in relationships that make us drop friends, change things around in our lives, and alter who we are slightly because the person we're with consumes us or all of our time. These are all lessons in love. And even when times get tough, there are things that we can learn from loving the wrong person.

While Kail has gone through relationships as we all have, hers are played out in front of the world. I can't imagine how challenging it must be at times to have people feel that they have a right to your personal affairs. Even though she is in the public's eye, she has not allowed that to sway who she is and what she wants for herself and for the boys.

Living under the microscope for so long has just become a part of her life. People can be brutal, but she is tough. She's been in this world of entertainment for ten years and deals with it well for the most part. We are all reminded that sometimes people tend to forget that she is human and that she has feelings too.

As Kail's friend, I sometimes have people say things to me that are not always favorable. Over time you learn not to let anything bother you. We are smart enough to know that the reaction of people is not something that we can control. Furthermore, none of it is a real reflection of her, it's more so about the person who chooses to slander on social media or other outlets.

The only time that I witness her get upset is when words are negatively spoken about her kids, which is understandable. Comments directed at her, she deals with, but when they're directed at those whom she loves, it can be hurtful. No matter how her path to discovering love has evolved, there has been one area of love in which she has never wavered: loving as a mother.

For as long as I've known her, Kail has been a steady force with her kids. She loves her kids without question, and they love her too. The chemistry and communication they have with each other are amazing to watch. Giving every ounce of her love as a mother is not who she has evolved into; she's been like that for as long as I've known her. She would do anything for the boys. It's nice to see that she's hard on them for things that matter. She doesn't want them to think that life is easy. She doesn't want them to believe that everything goes according to plan. She wants them to work for everything they have and to understand respect and fairness. I really admire her for this because a lot of people don't take time to ensure that their children have value for these areas of life.

If you watch these boys interact with each other, you'd quickly recognize that they love each other so much. They enjoy spending time with each other, and their sense of brotherhood is solid. They of course fight like brothers do, but they miss each other when not together. Kail does a good job trying to meet the different needs of each of the boys, and she really keeps them collectively together in love.

I will always love Kail, and appreciate the friendship we have that continues to grow. My greatest hope for her is that she discovers the happiness she deserves and a love that is respected mutually. She deserves this, as do we all.

I've known Kail for seven years, maybe longer, and I must say that our friendship has witnessed many lessons in so many different aspects of life. In the end, the most significant lessons learned have been in love. Love is all we have and all we need.

A Friend Always,
Becky Hayter

About the Author

Kailyn "Kail" Lowry is a television personality, book author, parenting blogger, and social media influencer with over eight million combined followers. She runs a website under her name, focusing on DIY, cooking, gifting, kids, and many relevant topics. Kail shares beloved personal and family photos on-site and via social; she frequently incorporates product and brand mentions therein.

Kail earned her Bachelor's Degree in Mass Communications from Deleware State University. She continues to evolve personally and professionally as the Host of Coffee Convos, a podcast dedicated to candid conversation and as the Founder and CEO of Pothead Inc., a newly launched hair care product line.

Arriving in the public eye via MTV's hit TV show *Teen Mom 2*, Kail quickly became one of America's favorite young moms. Kail is now a mother of three and a New York Times best-selling author.

CONNECT WITH

Kailyn Lowry

Contact: Info@kaillowry.com

Website: kaillowry.com

Instagram: @KailLowry

Lightning Source UK Ltd.
Milton Keynes UK
UKHW040207031220
374527UK00001B/109